BENSCREEK, PENNSYLVANIA

a memoir

by
Sophia Barnish

Copyright © 2013 Sophia Barnish
All rights reserved.

Published and edited by
Robert Leon Casey, JD

This is a memoriam by the author and some characters and events depicted in this book may be fictitious. Any similarity to actual persons, living or dead, is purely coincidental.

Cover photograph of Sophia Barnish
by John Barnish:
Mount Union Country Club,
Mont Union, Pennsylvania
August 6, 1950

Book block text and cover photo digitizing
by Jonathan Van der Mei

Contents

The Seventh Child 1

Three For The Road 21

Of Camels and Cheops 31

A Different World 39

Let Me Pass 57

Coal Miner Bus 63

Back To Benscreek 71

Mother of Heroes 81

The Polish Festival 87

Autumn Pilgrimage 93

Family Lineage 114

This memoir is dedicated to:

Donna Lynne Iding, my daughter
and her daughters, my granddaughters,
Heather Lynne and Melanie Ann

&

Robert Leon James Casey, JD, my son

&

My mother, Maryanna Czajka Barnaś, and
my father, Jan Barnaś

&

Brother Frank Barnish, his wife, Grace
and children
Frank, Betty, Janet, Dorothy, James

&

Sister Anna Barnish Weshalek

&

Sister Catherine Barnish Zajdel, her husband
John Zajdel
and sons Casimir, Thomas, Alan

&

Sister Rose Barnish Yanik, her husband
Joseph Yanik
and children Gloria, Joyce, David

&

Brother Joseph Barnish, his wife Ruth
and daughters Jo Nan and Peggy Lee

&

Brother John Barnish, his wife Helen
and children Rick, Mary, Michael

&

Sister Mary Barnish Caucci, her husband
Medio Caucci
and children Medio, Barry, Marina

&

Brother Stanley Barnish, his wife Joan
and children Margo, Christopher, Athena

The Seventh Child

The cold wind howled around the tiny frame home in the Allegheny Mountains, blowing February snow into high drifts against the front door and porch. Inside, hot coals crackled with a warm glow in the black cast iron stove in the corner of the kitchen. Maryanna was wet with perspiration and tried to suppress a cry of pain. The pains were coming faster now, closer and closer together. Mrs. Fetchik, the midwife, gently wiped Maryanna's forehead with a soft white towel and held her hand tightly. That wintry night, many years ago, Maryanna gave birth to her seventh child. The child was named Sophia. I am that child.

By 1932, my mother, Maryanna, would give birth to nine children. The tiny frame home with the cast iron stove in the village of Benscreek, just down the road from Portage, Pennsylvania, was witness to the births of the four youngest children, as well as one stillborn child.

Maryanna Czajka and Jan Barnaś, my mother and father, met in Chicago at a friend's wedding. Anglicized, Jan is equivalent to John. Both of my parents were born and raised near the town of Ochotnica, in the northern foothills of the Carpathian Mountains in what is now southern Poland, but they had not known each other until they met in America. Although Poland was established as a state in the year 966, my parents left their homeland when the area was called the Kingdom of Galicia, an autonomous region of the Austro-Hungarian Empire.

Poland once again became an independent country in 1918, at the conclusion of the First World War.

In April of 1903, father sailed out of Europe from Hamburg, Germany, aboard the *S.S Patricia*. He arrived at Ellis Island, New York Harbor, on April 17. According to the ship's manifest, list number 10, passenger number 7, Jan Barnaś, was 20 years old and had $30.00 in his pocket. In today's world, that's about $800.00. Not bad for a 20-year-old kid. He was to meet his cousin Wojciech Leszko in Pennsylvania.

It is believed that mother arrived in America in 1911 in Baltimore, Maryland. She was 17 years old. Mother and father soon married in Chicago and moved to Pennsylvania. Father was almost 14 years older than mother and found steady work as a coal miner in west-central Pennsylvania.

Mother named her first two sons, Frank and Joseph (who were separated by the births of three daughters, Ann, Catherine, and Rose), after Emperor Franz Józef of the Austro-Hungarian Empire. She remembered her mother telling her when she was a little girl in Poland that Franz Józef was kindly and considerate to his Polish-Galician subjects during the partitioning of Poland.

When mother's and father's first son, my oldest brother, Frank, entered the little four-room schoolhouse to begin 1st grade, his teacher, Miss Philomena Sheehan, asked him his last name. Understandably, he didn't know how to spell it; my brother simply said, *Barnaś*. Because the *s* of Barnaś has an accent mark above it, the *s* is pronounced as an *sh* sound. The teacher spelled it, *Barnish*. Miss Sheehan was the first teacher for six of the Barnish children: Rose, Joseph, John, Sophia, Mary, and Stanley.

When I returned to college in the late 1970s to get my degree, I was told by Dr. Jan Wilmanowicz, my Polish language professor, a Doctor of Languages, that Barnaś is not a Polish or Slavic name, it is a Scandinavian name. Perhaps that is why father had blue eyes and some of his children had blue eyes and blond hair. Several years ago, my son was given the same information by a woman from Sweden.

My earliest recollections were of my father playing the violin. My mother had bought it for him from the Sears Roebuck catalogue. He played lively Polish songs, while my mother smiled with happiness. Friends visited him on Saturdays, and they danced and sang. I would sneak some of the black coffee, laced with whiskey, which they drank. I thought it was horrid. This is likely the reason that I do not drink alcoholic beverages! I do, however, love coffee. I have a cup every day. Sometimes two. Or three.

I also remember the Christmas season when I was little. A few days before every Christmas, my father and brother Frankie would trudge off into the woods behind our house and chop down a small evergreen tree. They would come home panting and exhausted with our Christmas tree. The scent of pine would fill our little house. We decorated the tree with shiny metal icicles and some colorful glass ornaments which someone had given my mother many years before I was born. We all sat in the living room and were so happy, thinking we had the best life of anyone. Later, we went upstairs to bed, tired and contented. No one in our town ever mentioned the fabled visitor with the red suit as it was the Depression Era and little children were not entertained with that story.

Christmas in our house meant delicious walnut rolls and poppy seed rolls which my mother baked. The kitchen was filled with the heavenly aroma of the loaves in the oven. Later, when our entire family was seated around the festive table, we shared opłatki, thin Polish wafers, and wished each other good health and a long life. We had pan fried crusty fish, with cooked mushrooms in homemade sour cream. My father picked the mushrooms from the woods nearby and hung them on a string to dry by the stove. We all loved mashed potatoes and corn right out of our garden. Then came the best part of the Christmas Eve Vigilia dinner for my younger brother Stanley, my younger sister Mary and me. We each got a Chocolate Drop, a large delicious sweet from the grocery store, bought only once a year.

Speaking of candy, I remember a man named Mr. Fiszorek. I recently spoke about him with my younger sister, Mary, and she remembers him too. He was a bachelor friend of Father's. One day he visited our home with a paper poke of candy. Inside that paper bag there were all kinds of hard candy, even B B Bats -- all flavors, banana, strawberry, lemon, vanilla and chocolate. It was unbelievable! It was one of the happiest days of my childhood. You might say I have a sweet tooth.

I have such a vivid memory of the Tea Salesman, a man dressed in a suit and tie. He would come to our house and ask Mother if she would buy a little box of tea. It was the Depression, and, of course, there was not a dime to spare. Mother was so tender-hearted and felt sorry for him, so she would give him a cup of coffee and a slice of butter bread. I often wondered how far he walked in those Pennsylvania hills, dressed in his best clothes, in the heat of summer. I remember him to be a tall, good looking old man. Which meant that he was probably in his twenties. When we're children, we think anyone over 20 years of age looks ancient. I hope he had a happy life.

I also recall that someone gave Mary a doll when she was a little girl. It had blue eyes that opened and closed, just like Mary, and it had blonde hair, just like

Mary. I wasn't the least bit interested in dolls. I used to cut out the little girl models in the Sears Roebuck catalogue and give them names: Shirley Temple, Jane Withers, Marcia Mae Jones, Deanna Durbin. Then I pretended I was their teacher. I made sure I didn't play favorites and I never used a paddle.

In a few years, it was time for me to go to the Benscreek Elementary School, grades one through eight.

In the first grade, I was in a Christmas play and mother came to see me. She was very proud. I had to say a few lines and pretend that I was sewing something. I had to have a needle in my hand, which I thought was absurd – who in the audience would see a needle in my hand? The only line I still remember is, "See how fast my needle sews." I made a sewing motion as I said this. I had already lost the needle backstage, so I just moved my hand. No one was the wiser.

My first crush was Buddy Coffee in second grade. One morning, Buddy walked with me to school and said, out of the blue, "When we get married, I'll buy you a pair of silk stockings." Well, this certainly sounded to me like a marrying proposal. My happy future was assured. I was compelled to return his bold romantic overtures with my own bold move. On a piece of brown butcher paper, I printed *I Love You* and put the paper between two flat rocks at the corner fence post of his house. I'm 87 years-young now, and because I haven't heard from him in years, I'm pretty sure Buddy never discovered that correspondence placed between those rocks. Consequently, ours was a star-crossed future.

School was my passion. I received *Certificates of Perfect Attendance* through most of the grades, with the exception of the years I had chicken pox and measles. I wouldn't miss school even if I had a grinding toothache. My mother and father were very proud of me when they found out that I was promoted from the 5th grade to the 7th grade.

I remember standing by the coal stove on a cold February morning when Mother cut up a page from the Sunday Comics to make a pattern to fit me and sew a dress for my 7th birthday. The material had a yellow and white background. It had little red cherries and tiny hatchets on it. This was to honor both George Washington's birthday and mine, February 22.

Mother was an excellent seamstress and could do wonders with what little we had. With four sons and five daughters in our family, my mother did her best to sew clothes for all of us. She even sewed long-sleeved shirts for my four brothers. But our one pair of shoes and stockings had to last the entire school year.

All the girls wore the same dress for the entire five days of the school week. Then, on the weekend, our mothers would wash and iron the dresses. The same dress would be worn to school the following week. Some of us girls had older sisters and sometimes we were able to fit into their dresses as they were only a year or two older than we were.

All the girls wore the same dress to school every day of the week except Rita Zanuck, that is. Rita Zanuck was the best dressed girl in the whole school and the only one who wore two different dresses during the week to school. And Rita Zanuck had a tendency to stare. Usually at my dress and my shoes. I always tried to look unconcerned whenever Rita came to a stop a few feet away from me and stared. I was glad my brown ribbed stockings were pulled way down into my shoes so that she wouldn't notice the heavy white butcher cord with which my mother had repaired the holes in the heels of my stockings.

Rita riveted her eyes first on my faded and mended gingham dress, then slowly moved her glance downward at my stockings. Finally, with pretended disbelief, her mouth and eyes opened wide as she stared at my brown oxfords. She let out a shriek of laughter. "Look at Sophie's shoes! The cardboard is fallin' outta Sophie's shoes!"

Too timid to say anything and too embarrassed to be angry, I ran into the classroom. My face burned and, swallowing hard, I took my hankie and pretended to cough, but instead, wiped the stinging tears from my eyes.

Attending school during the Depression was challenging. And dumb girls can be complete bitches. I exacted my revenge by always getting the high grade in every class.

For the first few months of my freshman year at Portage Township High School, I walked the three miles distance. At the onset of winter, the Benscreek coal mine bus drove us to school. What unspeakable luxury! I scarcely noticed the coal dust clinging to the worn seats. No more would

I trudge through the snowstorms without boots, the freezing wind whipping through my cloth coat, my bones aching with the cold.

In high school we had a ping pong club and I was elected treasurer. For the championship title, I was pitted against Carl Montcalf. Since it was played during the lunch hour, there were several students looking on. After an especially vicious return, I saw my bra strap dangling out of the short sleeve of my blouse with a large safety pin attached to the end of it. I was horrified and ran out of the room and hid in a bathroom stall until the bell rang to signify the end of lunch hour. My buxom sister Rose had loaned me her old bra, with a pin attached to the broken strap. Heretofore I was bereft of the necessity of wearing one. Even though my score at that point in the game exceeded Carl's, he was declared the champion, which I didn't find out until I noticed it in the Yearbook months later. No one ever mentioned the aborted incident to me, for which I was grateful.

When I was a junior in high school, a few of my classmates and I were asked to be hostesses to seat the parents and friends of the graduating seniors. My mother was very shy and rarely left the house. But since I would be dressed in the lovely, pink bridesmaid gown I had worn to my sister Rose's wedding that year, my mother agreed to be driven to the Portage auditorium by my brother Frank to see me in my important role. As I proudly escorted my mother to a seat, she self-consciously sat down. But at that very moment, one of my female teachers came by and said, in a loud, officious tone, "She can't sit here, take her to the back! These seats are for the parents of the seniors!"

My mother died two months later, at the age of 45, because of a doctor's negligence. She was buried on the first day of my senior year of high school.

Somehow, and the reasons that I've heard don't make sense to me, mother developed a sore throat, which after a few days, only got worse. It was time to call a doctor. We never owned a telephone - owning a phone was an unaffordable luxury for our family and every family in the area. Consequently, my sister Ann went to the grocery store and called the nearest country doctor. He came to our house and suggested that mother have her tonsils removed. My sister Mary heard our father telling the doctor not to take them out. The doctor insisted and removed mother's tonsils at our house. It is likely his instruments were not sterile because her throat became severely infected.

I remember Mildred Oravecz parking her car on the dirt road in front of our house and father walking mother to the car. Mother was already yellowed with jaundice. We never owned a car, so Mildred drove mother and my oldest sister Ann to St. Mary's Hospital in Altoona. Mother died August 27, 1942, of septicemia. Blood poisoning. A few simple doses of penicillin would have saved her life. But penicillin was unavailable to most citizens because of World War Two, especially citizens of little means.

I have mother's wooden rocking chair in my bedroom. I often place my hand on the armrest and talk with her.

I was 16 years old when mother died, Mary was just 13, Stanley was only 10 years old. Because my other brothers and sisters were already out of the house, either married, working, or in the armed services, Mary and I had to wake up at 4:30 in the morning on alternate weeks to make the coal stove fire so father could have hot coffee before he walked to the coal mine. We made his minced ham (sliced bologna) sandwich for his lunch pail the night before, also an orange and a bun with icing. Coffee was kept in the inner container of the pail. His lunch was always the same.

The worst part of getting up so early on school days every other week was that Mary and I were so tired when we got to school, it was an effort to keep our eyes open and stay awake. During Latin class one day, Mr. Seymour asked me a question and I answered with a non-sequitur. He was a sympathetic and kindly professor who immediately ascertained that there had to be some upheaval in my life as it wasn't like me to mumble incoherently. Usually, I liked to speak up in class.

It was a beautifully sunny June day in the Pennsylvania hills when I completed my senior year at Portage Township High School. I was the valedictorian of my graduating class. When I gave the valedictory speech, my mother was not there. I wish she had been. She would have been so proud of her seventh child, the child she named Sophia.

Three For The Road

Driving in Michigan during the winter months when the roads are covered with snow and ice can test the skill of even the most confident driver. The simple act of backing out of a neighborhood driveway forces one to have the courage of a fighter-jet pilot entering the stratosphere.

On this particular February evening in 1969, I prepared to drive my daughter Donna Lynne to her ballet lesson at Flowery Dance Studio in Dearborn Heights. The drunken bum, I mean my husband, never seemed to find his way home after work until late at night, and tonight was no exception, so I would be tasked with the dance lesson driving duty. I took my young son Robert with us, not wanting to leave him alone at home for fear he'd demolish the place.

I guided the kids out the door and stepped outside. I was greeted with a frozen landscape. The streets were glazed with ice and the wind howled with a vengeance. I felt oncoming pangs of fear.

I feared what awaited me. In the midnight blue recesses of the detached garage it sat. Hiding in the shadows. And waiting. Waiting for me. Watching me.

The Corvair.

The maroon colored, 1961 Chevrolet Corvair Monza. The eight-year-old car that refused to run. The car that refused to stop. The car whose windows were always fogged and frozen. Even in the summertime. The aforementioned bum must have got a deal on it.

Thankfully, Ford Road was almost deserted after the dinner hour because of the inclement weather, but it was slick with ice. And I was certain that the other cars who actually were braving the frigid conditions were aiming their 4000-pound behemoths directly at my little car. Consequently, I crawled along at five miles an hour. I'm sure the other motorists were happy that I was so cautious. In fact, one driver surely must have recognized my careful driving technique, as he acknowledged it by wildly waving his upturned finger at me.

Fingers gripping the cold plastic steering wheel, I drove on. Hands positioned at ten-and-two, I peered past the dashboard and through the fogged windshield. I was determined to get Donna Lynne to the studio, as she was dedicated to her love of dancing and didn't want to miss a single class. We had phoned the young teacher and she told us she would not cancel the lesson as a few of the other students' mothers said they would certainly be there.

It was treacherous driving and I breathed a sigh of relief when we made it to the dance studio safely. When we walked into the studio, there was no one there except Miss Shaftstall, the instructor. She decided to wait another 15 minutes for the usual latecomers, but no one else came or even called. She gave Donna a private ballet lesson and Donna did splendidly, as she always did. But when it was time to leave, once again I felt oncoming pangs of fear. That blood-red demon would be waiting for me in the parking lot. My children and I walked out into the frigid, blustery night for the ride back home.

As there were no overhead street lights in the neighborhood, the night was pitch black when the three of us got to the parking lot behind the studio building. I forced the key into the partly frozen and barely obliging door lock, opened the doors, and we entered the refrigerated confines of the Corvair. The vinyl seats sent chills up our spines. I turned the key in the ignition.

Nothing.

My metal nemesis would not start. The headlights wouldn't even come on. Perhaps the battery was dead, too. Another joy to owning that maroon masterpiece-on-wheels was that the heater and defroster never did work. I could hear the echoes of my Corvair laughing an evil laugh.

I hoped there would be at least one person that might walk by whom I could call and beg for assistance to start my car, but to no avail. No one was out braving the arctic storm. The three of us began to shiver with the cold. I was terrified, and tried again to start that car.

My son told me "Mom, keep your foot on the accelerator longer, then let up, and do it again. But don't flood it."

"Okay," I said as my teeth chattered.

I had no idea what the term *flood* meant, or if I was or wasn't doing whatever it meant.

Suddenly, the Corvair let out a metallic belch of a sound and the engine came to life. I praised as many gods as I could think of. Donna and I were so thankful for our young automotive genius and his knowledge of floods. This is the boy who, when he was four years old, glued together a plastic car model without asking anyone for help. He said it was simple; he just looked at the drawings on the instructions to figure it out. I would still be trying to open the tube of glue.

But now I had to get us home in one piece. Not an easy thing to do when the outside surface of the car windows are glazed with

Three For The Road

ice. And when the mode of transportation has the leading role of the first chapter of the book *Unsafe At Any Speed*.

I rolled down my window to see how to get out of the parking lot, but the wind was vicious, and I rolled it back up. Ford Road was only a short distance away and there were a few stores with their lights on, but after a few miles I had to turn right on Inkster Road where it was dark and I could barely see to drive. So Donna and Robert kept telling me what side street I was passing as they kept trying to get the vapor off the inside of the windows. All three of us tried not to fog up the interior windows with our breathing as I crawled along. Finally they told me, "Mom, start turning your wheel to the left, Warren Avenue is right here." Next, they informed me after passing a few more side streets, "Turn your wheel now, Middlebelt Road is to the right."

A few minutes later, we were in our driveway. I parked the maroon miscreant in the garage. My brave children had helped me make the harrowing journey and we arrived safely home. We celebrated our victory with steaming cups of hot Ovaltine.

I had claimed victory over the Corvair.

Or had I? I thought I heard the demon whispering to me from out in the garage. Cloaked in darkness it hissed, "*Thursday night, Thursday night.*"

Thursday night was piano and guitar lessons for Donna and Robert.

Of Camels and Cheops

Powered by gaseous emissions fore and aft, the camel rose protestingly. First to his sand-encrusted knees and then slowly to his wide, padded feet. His appearance and demeanor matched the bleak Egyptian landscape with its sparse brownish-green vegetation and crumbling sandstone rock formations. From my precarious and uncomfortable seat on his single hump I could see the three Great Pyramids under a cloudless, blue Mediterranean sky. From half a world away, I had travelled to see our planet's oldest, largest and most enduring monuments of stone.

Holding tightly to the colorful scraps of yarn and rugs doubling as reins and saddle, I tried to look nonchalant and unconcerned sitting up there a mile high off the ground. Even though my camel's feet remained in one spot, his hump bobbed and undulated, making me feel as if I were in a miniscule boat on a choppy lake. I reminded myself that his single hump does store enough water for a long trek across the Sahara.

Now the lead driver shouted a command to the camel train. Not a single camel moved. Leaping off his mount, he struck the next camel in line and began screaming Egyptian epithets while kicking sand into the air with his sandaled feet. Accepting this noisy cue, the camels slowly and clumsily began the quarter mile trek uphill.

"Whoa, there, you varmint!" I attempted some cowboy rhetoric as my camel tried a few maneuvers that almost toppled me. Camels never throw their riders, I reassured myself as I tried to lie forward on the rough coarse hair of his bony neck. Of one thing I was certain, they never bathed. At that moment, as if reading my thoughts, the camel turned his head and looked at me with a baleful glare. "I'm sorry, pardner," I apologized; whereupon he responded with a defiant toss of his head and a warning, guttural sound deep inside his throat.

As our party wound slowly uphill, Egyptian boys, some of them as young as eight years old, rode expertly at great speed on beautiful Arabian horses. Shouting "Hi Yo, Silver!" and "Hubba Hubba!" they waved and smiled, showing white teeth in tanned, friendly faces as they tried to communicate in the only English they knew with the visitors from across the great ocean. Undoubtedly they had heard these words from their grandfathers who had fought in the African campaign of the Second World War.

At last we reached the top of the hill near the base of the Cheops Pyramid. Before we dismounted, my old gaudily dressed guide took a picture of me astride my camel to show the folks back home. I gave him a dollar. "Five mo' dulla!" he screamed. A dollar was enough, I told him. "Rich American!" he shrieked, "Five mo' dulla!" Telling me that I could stay up there on the camel forever, he rode away with my expensive camera. I yelled back at him, telling him he would lose his guide job when I got through with him as I knew the Minister of Tourism and President and Mrs. Sadat. Fearing for his job, he shouted a command to my camel, who began weaving back and forth in all directions of the compass and then banged down on his rump with such force that I was catapulted headfirst into the sand. Hearing shrieks of laughter, I looked up and saw my cowardly friends who had taken the bus instead of the camels uphill and were waiting for me near the entrance to the Cheops Pyramid.

Supposedly erected in the third millennium B.C. by a civilization that did not know of or use the wheel, the pyramid was accredited to the Pharaoh Cheops. The monstrous mound of limestone and granite rock sits on a thirteen-acre site. It is 481 feet high, with each side measuring 755 feet in length. Coming nearer, you can see the ravages wrought by treasure hunters seeking souvenirs, and quarriers who have gouged the sides of the pyramid, seeking stone to construct mosques and palaces in the city of Giza below and Cairo in the northeast.

Although the interior passageways were said to be lit by flaring torches that reflected their light off of mirrors of polished bronze, there are no traces of soot or ash on the ceilings of the interior tunnels. The immense structure is lit in this age by a few scattered electric bulbs.

Inside the corridor, you must bend your back as you walk upward along a high processional aisle which leads higher and deeper into the bowels of the pyramid. This is the Grand Gallery, an aisle without windows or pillars, with polished limestone walls. With every step you take, you are deeply conscious that the vaulted roof which is a few inches above your head has withstood the crushing weight of more than two million blocks of stone for almost five millennia. You come at last to the granite burial chamber of Cheops. But the sarcophagus, or flesh eater, as the Greeks called it, is empty. The mummified corpse of the pharaoh had long ago been mysteriously moved and the chamber robbed of its gold and precious artifacts. The theft was presumably perpetrated by the high priest, our guide told us, as he was the only one entrusted with the secret of the location of the burial chamber. The workers who had carried the sarcophagus had all been mysteriously poisoned.

After holding us enthralled with tales of palace intrigue in the pharaoh's court, the narrator led us out of the dark burial chamber. We carefully retraced our steps down the narrow passage. It seemed difficult to breathe inside this gigantic tomb. It was an immense relief to come back out into the brilliant Egyptian sunlight.

I was also immensely relieved to see that my plush travel accommodations had arrived. Standing squarely in front of me was my malignant-eyed camel, whose crooked lips and odor-emitting mouth chewed on some unknown cud. I was certain the furry, fly-magnet was smiling back at me.

I gave him a pat on his shoulder and said, "Well, hello there, pardner."

He burped and dutifully awaited my command to haul me back to the hotel bus at the bottom of the hill.

A Different World

In 1932, my oldest sister Ann boarded a train and took it all the way to Grand Central Station in New York City. She was 15 years old and she was headed to Brooklyn where she hoped to find work as a maid. Most of the girls in small towns in central Pennsylvania didn't go to high school because their parents considered them to be successfully educated once they completed the eighth grade. After all, in those days, it was almost a necessity that an American boy or girl in their mid-teens -- who had not been born with a silver spoon in their mouth -- should be working by that age in order to help their family survive the Great Depression. And although my father was a hardworking man, it was difficult to raise a family on the wage that the coal mines paid their miners.

By word of mouth, from town to town, the poor families of Pennsylvania let it be known to their friends and relatives that there was a need for young intelligent women to be maids and caretakers for the babies and young children of affluent families in the big city of New York. The five populous boroughs that make up the city of New York beckoned to the poor teenage girls of the Alleghenies.

My mother was worried that her first-born daughter would be living with complete strangers in a big city so far away and the possible misadventures which could accompany that circumstance. My oldest brother Frank reassured my mother that the daughters of many of our father's close friends had already been working for a few years in New York City.

Frank explained to my mother, "Just because a person is poor does not mean that that person is stupid. Poor people have the uncanny ability to learn quickly and better themselves, they are survivors. Ann is wise, but also gentle and kind. She will be fine, mother."

Several of Ann's friends in our tiny hometown of Benscreek, Pennsylvania, had already been hired and wrote to her, advising her of the events and rules of their gainful employment. They all seemed to truly enjoy their host family.

Ann told my mother and father that she was ready.

My family knew that it was time to let Ann travel to the city.

It was early April when Ann boarded the train in nearby Cassandra. Brooklyn awaited the arrival of my sister.

When Ann surmounted the stairways of Grand Central Station and stepped to the streets of New York City, what sights she must have seen! What differences in dress, in manners, in communication, in technology she must have witnessed. How did she feel when all she could see was a man-made mountain of cement and steel and glass? How did she sleep in the noisy din of that city? Did she find herself feeling as small as the little Pennsylvania town from which she hailed? Surely, Ann took it all in stride.

It was Mr. and Mrs. Weisbrot of Brooklyn who hired my sister to be their maid and caregiver to their son. The Weisbrots treated Ann with respect and kindness, as if she was part of their own happy family. They were so delighted with Ann's attention to detail and the way in which she calmly completed her tasks, that by

A Different World

August, they asked Ann if she would be willing to take their 7 year-old son, Larry, to our home in Benscreek for a week's vacation.

Ann was in awe of the responsibility, knowing that little Larry was so headstrong and vocal. Of course, that's normal for a seven-year-old boy. I was the same age, and I imagine that I was just as vocal. But, little Larry was also kind, loving, and adored Ann.

So one day in mid-August, our next-door neighbors in Benscreek, the Jadick brothers (all five of them: John, Paul, Joe, Steve and Andy) jumped into their old, four-door Tin Lizzie, otherwise known as a Ford Model T automobile, and left a trail of blue-white exhaust smoke all the way to the Cassandra train station, where they picked up Ann and Larry.

Now, it seems that Larry had never been out of the city. Larry was unbelievably excited, looking out the car windows and exclaiming, "Wow! Look at that cliff! That's a long way down! Is that a coal mine? Let me off here! I want to climb that big tree! Look at that horse!"

The horse was actually a dairy cow.

Well, Larry certainly enjoyed his one week vacation with us. He especially liked to climb trees and we couldn't keep him out of the swimming streams that wound their way among the tall shade trees of Benscreek.

Larry was overjoyed when the Benscreek kids his age asked him to join their ragtag baseball team. Even when he got a black eye after he misjudged an infield fly ball, he was very brave and tried not to cry. Little Larry even allowed Boonda Jadick, the nickname of the aforementioned Andy Jadick, the wheel-man of the smoking Tin Lizzy, take a photograph of him proudly displaying that black eye, just to show his mom and dad back in New York. The Jadicks rivaled my family in terms of income, or lack thereof, so I have no idea where Boonda got such a fancy thing as a camera.

Ann stayed with the Weisbrots in Brooklyn that winter, writing home every week.

Little Larry must have talked so much about his time in Benscreek that, the next summer, Mrs. Weisbrot came with Ann to our home and stayed for a week's vacation. Larry stayed with Mr. Weisbrot in Brooklyn. Luckily, we had a little room where Mrs. Weisbrot could look out on our beautiful grapevine. Mrs. Weisbrot said she loved the deep green color of the leaves that waved in the breeze. She admired the pink Morning Glories growing around the window and the scent from the blossoms of the lilac bush and Bleeding Hearts. I remember she made herself a lemon and hot water drink the first thing every morning. She called it a tonic or something similar. She wrote a letter to her husband and Larry every day.

One day, I sneaked into her little room and found a letter she had written to her husband. She had tossed it away, maybe to rewrite it. But, being that I read anything and everything I laid my hands on, I read it. It was so surprising that someone would waste their time to write about the weather – sunny, lovely, leafy, flowers, tree leaves dripping with dew! I was rather disappointed. When I wrote to my sister Ann in New York, I certainly didn't write about the weather, I wrote about important and weighty things, as I had much deeper thoughts and concerns. I would tell Ann to buy me a dress or send me a dollar. Well, I was, after all, only seven years old.

My sister Catherine, who liked to be called Kay, was two years younger than my sister Ann. When Kay finished the 8th grade, Ann wrote to her and said she would meet her at the Grand Central train station in New York City. So, now my two oldest sisters were in New York City, and I know that they were happy to be together. Ann took Kay to an employment office where

A Different World

Kay was immediately hired by a Mr. and Mrs. Goldstein. Kay took care of Betty, their infant girl.

The following summer, Mr. and Mrs. Goldstein actually asked Kay if she would take the infant Betty with her back to Benscreek and the Pennsylvania mountains for the fresh air while they vacationed in Miami. Kay brought Betty to our home and, since Betty was just a toddler, Kay wouldn't let her out of her sight. Kay and our mother fawned over the baby, and all the while she cooed and babbled her baby talk.

Now, I was young, but I was beginning to wonder why these New York people were always coming to my house in the mountains. I thought that it was time to pay a visit to New York City and see why all the rich folk were coming out to my little town of Benscreek, Pennsylvania.

After six years in Brooklyn, Ann was back in Benscreek, married to a local man. By the summer of 1939, Kay was still in Brooklyn taking care of little Betty Goldstein. I mentioned to Ann that I heard there was a World's Fair in New York, near Brooklyn. I was about to enter high school and not yet working, so Ann said she would give me train fare and thought that I might be able to stay for a few nights at the Goldstein's with Kay. So, it came to pass a week later that Ann and her husband drove me to nearby Cresson, handed me some pocket change, and put me aboard a Greyhound Bus to New York City.

For me, the bus ride was a painful misery. I had the worst headache and motion sickness. Busses in those days were not the plush rolling coaches that are seen today smoothly gliding over miles of superhighways. They were rattling, hulking behemoths that spewed more noxious fumes inside the bus than outside, making the hours-long trip on the hard-as-rocks seat unbearably uncomfortable. My ride seemed unending. I didn't sleep the entire night and watched the gray dawn appear with no sunshine, only a miserable rain pelting down against the windows.

The bus stopped for gas somewhere in New Jersey and the passengers got out near a little stand selling ice cream in tiny cardboard cups. When we all got back on the bus a few minutes later, I soon realized that I couldn't eat my ice cream. The vendor did not give me a little wooden spoon. Without ice cream, my head pounded all the more.

Finally, the monstrous metal ark arrived at Pennsylvania Station in New York City. I waited for Kay where Ann told me to wait, but I did not see my sister. I could not hope to find Kay in that immense, noisy station filled with loud and pushy people. People did not act this way in Benscreek. I wasn't sure what to do, so I sat on a wooden bench in the middle of the cavernous interior of the station.

And waited.

Where was Kay?

I waited some more.

I was young and naïve and must have looked like a fish out of water. Any smooth-talking New York playboy might have thought me an easy mark. But, I had a sharp tongue and a sharp mind, so I stayed alert to the surroundings. I could run pretty fast too.

To my joy, I heard Kay's voice calling, "Sophie! Sophie!"

She told me she had no idea I was coming to New York, but Mary Oravecz, her friend from the hamlet of Shoemaker, near Benscreek, also worked in Brooklyn and called Kay. She told Kay I was coming by Greyhound and would be at Pennsylvania Station. Kay had only found out just minutes before my arrival. Kay was frantic! Our sister Ann had forgotten to call Kay and tell her. It was fortuitous that a mutual friend in Benscreek had spoken

A Different World

by phone with Mary Oravecz in Brooklyn and, just as friendly gossip, had mentioned that I was to be in New York. Mary said something about it to Kay, and, after Kay had recovered from disbelief, she checked the bus arrival times, getting to the station at just the right moment. To this day I do not know how she found me in that huge station. If she had not, I might still be face-slapping some smooth-talking New York playboy.

Well, I was flabbergasted when I entered the lovely home of the Goldstein's. It was like a movie to me. A stove that miraculously cooked pies and potato pancakes without having to first ignite a piece of paper, then a twig, then a piece of coal in order to start a fire to do the cooking. The bathroom was sparkling with smooth tile and had a shiny toilet seat to sit down on. And no Sears Roebuck catalog for paper. There was a soft white roll of paper nearby, called toilet tissue. The tissue was sold in stores.

Shockingly, here at the Goldstein's, I slept by myself. I was used to sleeping with at least two of my siblings in one bed. I slept in a nice bed, with fancy sheets, in a room by myself. When Ann and Kay got to New York and first started working, they must have been in disbelief. Surely, they were happy to have a soft mattress, new sheets, and an entire bed to themselves. Perhaps, for a while, they were lonely and missed the camaraderie of their other sisters, but after writing a few letters home, and enclosing a five dollar bill for mother, they undoubtedly looked forward to many nights like this.

I pulled the white bed sheet around my shoulders. I thought about how Mrs. Weisbrot and Mrs. Goldstein must have felt when they visited my house in Benscreek. Our house was clean, we ate healthy food, and the hills of Pennsylvania were beautiful, but the house was without running water, electricity, central heat, a bathroom, a telephone, and our family did not own a car. Even as I drifted off to

A Different World

sleep, I missed my home, I missed mother and father, I missed my mountains.

The next morning, Kay took me to Thom McCann's and bought me a pair of white oxfords with tan saddles – saddle shoes. The City was so busy. I caught myself staring at just about everybody and everything. Then, Kay's boyfriend Arnie, a Jewish boy from a wealthy family, picked us up and drove the three of us to the World's Fair.

The 1939 New York World's Fair in the borough of Queens was a wonderful sight to behold, with lights flashing everywhere, and interesting exhibitions to experience. Some inventions and gadgets were too involved for me to understand at my age, but I was amazed by their movement and action. There were throngs of people there, all oohing and ahhing at the futuristic display of knowledge and technology.

Now, Arnie seemed like a nice enough guy to me, courteous and dressed in nice clothes. With Arnie's camera, Kay took a photo of me and Arnie standing in front of the General Electric building at the World's Fair. I was looking good in my new Thom McCann saddle shoes and powder blue silk dress with lace collar. I especially liked my dark blue velvet belt and matching navy blue jigger coat. I still have that black and white photo.

After three full days with Kay, I left the skyscrapers of New York City and headed back to Benscreek. Fortunately for me, I traveled by train this time. Mrs. Goldstein was nice enough to insist that I was comfortable for my trip back and told Kay that she could have a week off in order to accompany me. Mrs. Goldstein paid for our train tickets.

Kay worked one more year in Brooklyn and then came back to Benscreek, married a good man, and had a family. I finished high school as the valedictorian in 1943.

Both of my sisters lived and worked in New York for over five years. They had grown from teenage girls to beautiful young adult women by the time they returned to Benscreek. I was happy that I had the opportunity to visit Kay while she was there. Even though Ann, Kay, and I all experienced the shine and glamor of the big city of New York, not one of us made the decision to live our lives there. Why not? Just like the Weisbrots and Goldsteins, who loved their week-long escapes to our country home, maybe we too knew that Benscreek, Pennsylvania, our little jewel in the mountains, was much more special than any man-made mountain of cement, and steel, and glass.

Let Me Pass

I was terror stricken. My heart contracted with fear when I saw the two strangers blocking my way at the top of the deserted stairs. Did I only imagine their menacing smiles? Why did I come to the movies alone in this unfamiliar neighborhood so late at night? My thoughts raced in kaleidoscopic fashion to the events preceding this dilemma. I vowed never again to venture alone if I ever got out of this frightening experience unharmed.

It was one of those days when one was filled with a sense of accomplishment. My day at the office was busy and satisfying; I finished my assignments and said goodnight to my co-worker girlfriend Helen. My piano lesson at the Detroit Institute of Arts made me feel as if I were really a descendant of Chopin; and later, while shopping, I found a beautiful little organdy dress to send to my new niece in Pennsylvania. All in all, it was a happy and rewarding day. Glancing at my watch, I noticed that it was eight o'clock, but, being July, it was still light out-of-doors.

I boarded a Woodward streetcar for my return home. Sitting there, watching several young couples laughing, and obviously looking forward to the plans they had made for the evening, I decided that I was in no hurry to get back to my small, rented room. I was twenty-one years old and suddenly felt very lonely.

As the streetcar rumbled on, I noticed a marquee proclaiming the showing of WAGES OF FEAR and, in smaller letters, informing the public that the movie was the Winner of the Cannes Film Festival. I pulled the signal cord and the driver soon came to a stop. After buying my movie ticket, I found a seat near the center aisle. The theater was small, sparsely attended, with mostly couples who were engaged in various forms of petting and lovemaking. An old man snored with his mouth open.

WAGES OF FEAR, with Yves Montand, proved to be a suspenseful film, depicting the slow, tortuous journey of two trucks loaded with nitroglycerine and their gut-wrenching passage over precipitous mountain roads in South America. Almost every turn in the road presented a new obstacle. Each truck was tensely piloted by two men who had to deliver the explosive cargo to an oil field that was burning out of control.

I was so engrossed in this superb film that I didn't realize until the final scenes that I was sitting there alone. Everyone else had left the theater.

I left my seat and, as the restrooms were on the second floor of the tiny theater, made my way up a narrow carpeted stairway to find the powder room. When I came back out, I looked down the short hallway and saw two young adult men standing on each side of the entranceway to the very narrow stairs. Their legs and feet were extended in front of them, creating an obstacle course of sorts, and barricading my passage. They looked at me and smiled. At that moment, I felt as apprehensive as the four men in the film who held their breath and nervously handled the nitroglycerine.

I came nearer, but the young men didn't move their feet at all, they just kept smiling at me.

Let Me Pass

With a calm expression on my face, I turned back a few steps toward the restroom and said in a loud voice, "I'll wait for you downstairs, Helen!"

I slowly walked between the two young men, who moved their feet ever so slightly to let me pass.

I walked out of the theater without looking back and hailed a taxi for my ride home. I wonder if those boys are still waiting for Helen to emerge from the restroom.

Coal Miner Bus

The last time I put pen to paper, I regaled you with the cultural news of my school years. You might recall Georgie Bruschin, his infamous hand mirror, and how he angled it so that he could see up Ellen Obshefsky's dress as she demurely sat in class. So, not wishing to stray from that renowned gentleman's acclaimed performances, let me entertain you with an event from 1939.

I was thirteen, and a proud scholar of the Freshman Class of Portage Township High School. Thirteen? Yes, I went from fifth grade to seventh, so I was young when I got to high school.

One morning, I ran across the ball diamond and boarded the Benscreek Coal Miner Bus on its way to Springhill, a suburb of Portage. The Coal Miner Bus not only took the local coal miners to the local mines, but it let the local kids get free rides to school, including the township high school, which was in Springhill.

I clambered up the coal dust encrusted step and into the Coal Miner Bus. I was still searching for a clean seat when a loud, raucous voice greeted me. It was Georgie.

"Hey, Sophie, Eddie Musial told me you wouldn't let him touch yer tits!"

Horrorstricken, I blindly groped for a seat. I don't remember the rest of the bus ride to school. I do remember thinking it now made sense why Georgie and Eddie had always acted like goofy and gangly boys when they were around me.

The next day, I had recovered from the shock, but still I pondered my dilemma of facing that cohort of coal bus rapscallions. I boarded the Coal Miner Bus, ignored the knowingly smirking bus driver, and said to Georgie very sweetly, "Georgie. I do so appreciate your comment yesterday confirming my virtuous behavior." My grammar easily baffled the young man.

Now, I must tell you that the entertainment and nightlife in little Benscreek, Pennsylvania, was lacking in excitement, possibly even nonexistent. And, since I had never brought a schoolbook home to while away the evenings, I was usually bored stiff when I wasn't in school. Aside from the occasional spat with my brother Johnny or my sister Mary, life to me was duller than staring at the local Rock Dump. So, as was my wont, I put on my brown oxfords and walked up the road to my sister Ann's house.

Now, in our idyllic village, not far from the grade school, lived the aforementioned Eddie Musial and his family. My sister Ann's husband, who worked as the butcher in the grocery store, told me that Eddie thought I was the Cat's Meow. Well, that's a big deal for 1939. But I hardly knew Eddie, except for the fact that Mr. Mackey, the Principal and teacher of all the subject matter for my seventh and eighth grades, often called on Eddie to go to the blackboard, and, when exasperated with his inaccurate mathematical conclusions, would deliver a swift kick to Eddie's blue jeans. I remember admiring Mr. Mackey's shiny black shoes as they arced gracefully to their target.

I digress. When I got to my sister Ann's house, I sat on her front porch swing. I was alone, but not lonely. It was a lovely, moonlit night, with a gentle breeze ruffling my straight bangs.

I pretended I was astride Silver, behind the Lone Ranger, and we sang,

Oh, give me land, lots of land,
Under starry skies above,
Don't fence me in!

I had my eyes closed as I sang.

Let me ride through the wide,
Open country that I love,
Don't fence me in!

All of a sudden, I felt a thud, and to my distaste, as the image of the Lone Ranger faded, it was replaced by the presence of Eddie Musial.

Without a proper invitation from me, he rudely sat down next to me on the swing, disrupting my romantic reverie. He tried to put his arm around me, but, with a piercing scream, I leaped off the swing in midair and streaked into my sister's house.

Ann immediately came to the door of the porch. "What on earth is going on here? I thought someone was being murdered!"

"Honest, Mrs.Weshalek. I just tried to put my arm around her. I didn't do anything wrong."

"I believe you, Eddie," Ann said. "Otherwise Sophie would have ripped your eyes out of your head."

My sister knew me well.

Back To Benscreek

After I graduated high school, I took a train to Detroit. My sister Ann was already there and said I would be able to easily find employment. I worked for Dodge Motors as a stenographer (I have no idea how I passed the shorthand test), and then as an executive secretary in the Chrysler Export Division.

Ann soon moved back to Pennsylvania which left me without family in Detroit. Thanksgiving Day and Easter Sunday were lonely holidays for me back in

Michigan. My fellow workers talked happily about the delicious feasts their mothers were preparing and the family members who were due to arrive. I lived alone in a tiny rented room far away from the only home I knew and far away from the family I loved. I was questioning my decision to move to Detroit.

With every paycheck, I mailed money to father. My father was becoming stooped and arthritic from years of bending in a coal mine, and I was determined to make his days less burdensome. I was happy to send money home so that my younger sister Mary and my little brother Stanley would have warm clothes for school. But it was so sad for me to know that Mary, so young, had to do the many backbreaking chores that Mother used to do, with just a few hours of sleep, while I was so far away in another state, with no housework and a comfortable job. In the spring of 1945, I decided to go back to Pennsylvania and look for a job near home to help take care of Father, Mary, and Stanley.

I arranged my vacation time from Chrysler and took the train from Detroit back to Benscreek. My brother Johnny was home on leave for a few days after basic training. He was anxious to show me what he learned in the Marines. He lined up a few empty cans on the railroad track at the bottom of the hill below our house, and asked me if I wanted to watch him shoot them all down. We stood on the hill and he proudly exhibited his skill with the rifle as one by one, the cans flew up into the air. It looked exciting to me. He let me take a turn and I shot two cans. He couldn't believe that I did it on my first try. I told him he was a good teacher; I did what he told me to do—just close one eye and line up the sights with those cans down there on the rails, don't move, and squeeze the trigger. Simple! I was ready to join the Marines and started to sing the words, "From the Halls of Montezuma to the shores of Tripoli," from one of my favorite songs, *The Marines Hymn*.

Afterwards, I freshened up, threw on a little makeup, and decided it was time to look for a job. The Benscreek mine where my father worked was my first stop. I walked up the tracks opposite the mine tipple and entered the dark and dingy office of the coal mine. There were three elderly lady employees sitting at their desks. They looked surprised to see a young girl with high heels and the latest fashion of dress.

"Are you hiring?" I politely asked.

"Hiring for what?"

"A receptionist."

"A receptionist? At a coal mine?" one old bird chirped, obviously forgetting to smile.

"Or an office manager?" I asked.

"We don't need an office manager," another dowdy matron snorted.

Well, I thought, this is going well.

I thanked the old biddies and exited.

It was a warm sunlit day, so I went back to the house and sat on the front porch swing with Mary and Father.

Father was very fond of all his four sons and talked proudly of them. Frank was a sergeant and a dental technician in the Army. Joe was in the Navy in World War II and was also a paramedic in the Korean conflict. He trained the younger soldiers to jump from airplanes to help the wounded on the battlefield. Years later, we found out that, after Korea, Joe was a CIA agent. My brother John, who was only a year and a half older than I, was a rifle marksman and bayonet expert in the Dragon III Division in the Marines. He was honorably discharged after being wounded in action with the enemy at the battle at Eniwetok in the Pacific. At 13 years of age, Stanley was much too young to join the military service, but became a whiz at designing and crafting woodwork and repairing all the necessities around the house.

I casually asked where Stanley was. Mary said that he walked to Jamestown with his buddies, Johnny Rocker and Leo Holiday and Leo Spodnik and would probably end up in Portage to see more of their friends. Then she said, "He has a Clubhouse in the shanty near the stone wall." I was amazed and thought, *What has time wrought?* My precious little brother is growing up.

Father smiled knowingly.

Mary and I went to see Stanley's Clubhouse. I opened the door, and who should be there smiling coyly at me but Marilyn Monroe! The brazen hussy had not a stitch of clothing on! I noticed that Stanley had strategically hung the calendar on a nail to be the focal point of his hideout. I could well imagine his gleeful anticipation as he invited all his many friends to view his new hangout. Well, no longer could I talk to Stanley as if he were a little boy. He was a normal teenager!

The next day, I returned to my quest for hometown employment. Undaunted by the previous day's encounter with the three hell-hounds, I walked the two and a half miles to Portage. On Main Street, I entered Schoenfield Department Store. No one was there, except one gentleman who turned out to be the manager. Even though he didn't smile to put me at my ease, he was honest and considerate. When I told him I now worked at Chrysler World Headquarters but I would like to come back home to Benscreek to help my Father and sister and little brother, he did not say there were no jobs available, but he asked me what salary I received. When I told him, he whistled and said, "You can help your father more by going back to Detroit and send money home. You could not earn that here."

Well, that encounter cemented the reality of it all. The big cities paid more than any rural American town. I returned to Detroit and continued to send money to the family that I loved.

Father eventually moved in with my sister Kay and her husband John in their house outside of Lilly. He happily lived out his days. After working for years in one of the most physically demanding jobs in the world, and successfully raising a big family, he died on May 7, 1962, at 79 years of age.

Mother of Heroes

It was a glorious winter day in January. President and Madame el Sadat had left Koubbeh Palace in Cairo and were on a brief vacation in the south of Egypt. At the invitation of a mutual friend, Mostafa Afr, a few of us were honored to visit the Sadats at their country home in Aswan, a few miles north of the Sudanese border. After showing our credentials to the bayonet-bearing guards who lined the circular drive in front of their hilltop residence, we were given permission to enter the estate.

Madame Jehan Sadat graciously greeted us with a warm and lovely smile. "Welcome to Egypt," she said. "I hope you are enjoying our wonderful weather." Her voice was soft, with traces of a French accent. Of medium height, about 5'5", she wore her auburn hair in a soft wave about her face. Her complexion was a tawny beige and her long nails were tinted to match the fashionable magenta afternoon dress she wore. A double strand of pearls encircled her throat.

We walked with her through the flower-bedecked trellis, down a few marble steps, and to a sunken garden. A few yards away, the Nile River flowed majestically. The air was perfumed with the exotic scents of vividly hued flowers which grew in profusion about the spacious lawn. Birds with brilliant plumage perched in the orange, lemon and mango trees. It was a perfect setting for our charming hostess. Jehan, the Egyptians say, is more beautiful than was Cleopatra, lovelier even than Nefertiti, their favorite queen.

On long tables spread with white linen, servants set before us chilled tropical drinks, with heaping platters of beef, lamb, chicken, seafood, vegetables, fruits and tantalizing trays of luscious desserts.

Jehan Sadat seated herself among us and said, "Anwar and I are happy that you have come to share our day. You see he is there taking a meeting in the gazebo, and he will be unable to join us for lunch." As she spoke she waved her arm in her husband's direction. He returned her wave, nodded in our direction, and resumed his private conversation. "Anwar is consulting with his foreign affairs minister, as Menachem Begin is due to arrive here tomorrow for peace talks."

She conversed with us about her family; her two older daughters were attending English literature classes at Cairo University, and her younger daughter was still in secondary school. Her son Gamal was studying Engineering and was an ardent amateur pilot. Her hobbies included books, music, tennis and swimming. At night, she walked with her husband and children for an hour of exercise on the grounds of the estate.

"My days are busy, but fulfilling," she continued. "I am most proud of my official title, 'Mother of Heroes.' I visit at least one hospital every day. It is heartbreaking to see our young men lying in their beds, some unable to ever walk again. They are mostly mere boys in their late teens and early twenties. They cry when they see me. They miss their homes, their mothers. I put my arms about them and comfort them. I tell my husband, 'Please, Anwar, tell the leaders of Israel and the Arab nations to stop this incessant fighting; they must compromise.' Our money should be used to build schools, roads and hospitals. Anwar is doing everything possible to ensure a just and lasting peace with the Arab world. And I am most interested in the rehabilitation and retraining of our disabled war veterans."

Jehan Sadat continuously fights to better the under-privileged position of women in Egypt. "Through my efforts there are improved opportunities in education and training and a reform of the divorce law. Western-style emancipation is not what we strive for. Our women must be aware of and acknowledge the uniqueness of the country from which we come, because each Middle East country has its own special ways which are rooted in its social and moral traditions. This is why the women of Egypt must not blindly copy the ways of the women of other countries, but must continue to create a path that is true to our specific needs."

After two hours of delightful conversation, Mrs. Sadat's secretary reminded her of her next appointment. Prior to her departure, Jehan Sadat graciously allowed me to have a picture taken with her. As she slipped her arm through mine, she whispered, "Thank you for the love and friendship you bring to Egypt."

The Polish Festival

"Jak sie masz, Stas'?"
"Dzien dobry!"
"Let's go to the Oaza Bakery and buy some pączki."

It is the Labor Day Festival in Hamtramck, Michigan. On this day, the city honors all men and women for their diligent commitment to ensuring that the government and the lives of all citizens will be running harmoniously. The main street of Hamtramck, Joseph Campau Avenue, is thronged with people of all ages enjoying the festive atmosphere. They have come from the neighboring suburbs, and even from out of state, in order to reunite with their friends and relatives. Some have come all the way from Poland, planning their vacation to coincide with this holiday. All have come to enjoy the camaraderie, the tasty cuisine, and the Polish Labor Day Parade.

"Here come the fire trucks!" a little boy shouts.

Everyone scatters from Joseph Campau and lines up along the sidewalk to watch. Little girls and boys, holding aloft their balloons of yellow, green, red and white, begin waving excitedly to the firemen, who happily return their waves. There are fire trucks representing the cities of Detroit, Royal Oak, Highland Park, and, of course, Hamtramck. The hometown brigade receives a thunderous ovation in several languages. Bells clanging and whistles shrieking, the firemen proudly drive their trucks down the thoroughfare.

The Polish Festival

Old and young alike enjoy the shiny, red fire trucks with sirens screaming.

Next come the high school bands, with drums beating, and trumpets blaring. Looking lovely in their short, swirling, colorful outfits, the majorettes leap and smile as they twirl and toss their batons high into the air and gracefully catch them again. The cheer leaders smile and wave to their friends and families, with teachers and boyfriends all happily looking on. Their talents and lovely appearance do not go unnoticed by the young men, from eight to eighty, who whistle in appreciation as they prance and glide by.

Next, a beautiful, flower-bedecked float drives slowly by. Miss Hamtramck, standing on the float and clutching an armful of American Beauty roses, waves to her adoring throng, bestowing on them her dazzling smile.

Finally, after several slow-moving limousines drive by, occupied by local dignitaries, the governor's shiny black limousine drives by. He shouts a few words in Polish to the delight of the laughing and applauding crowd. The governor's car is the final car of the motorcade. Joseph Campau Avenue is once again open for all to enjoy.

Now, everyone rushes over to the food stalls for some wholesome old time Polish cuisine. The food is kept hot and sizzling on the stoves of each chef.

Passing by the bakery, I succumb to the tantalizing aroma of the kruszcziki (angel wings), pączki, and nut rolls. I walk in, take a number, and get ready for the long wait in a line that doubles around twice inside the bakery, with customers still trying to come in, but now starting to form a line outside of the door.

Standing there, my mind wanders back to my childhood, and I vividly remember Sunday suppers when my Mother placed steaming hot plates of kiełbasa, sauerkraut and mashed potatoes on the table, with horseradish and thick slices of homemade bread. Borne on the wings of memory, I loudly smack my lips right there in the bakery. The elderly gentleman in front of me turns and says, "Rozumiem." (I understand)

Autumn Pilgrimage
Back To My Hometown

WELCOME TO PENNSYLVANIA the sign over the Turnpike greeted us. My sister Mary and I were elated. "Pennsylvania!" we shouted in unison. Our love for the state of our birth has never diminished.

Now, after driving so many miles, we were exhilarated by the gorgeous panoramic view of the Alleghenies. All around us, majestic trees with leaves of russet and gold shimmered in the autumn wind as sunbeams danced on their branches.

Mary reminded me, "Exit 6 is coming up, don't forget to get off the Turnpike." After several miles on Route 22, we spied a cardboard sign on the side of the road which proclaimed *Farm Produce 4 Sale*. Our weekend goal was to get to our sister Kay's house, then walk the wooded hills of Benscreek, the town of our birth, but this roadside enticement seemed like a worthwhile interruption.

"Let's stop to see what the farmer has for us!"

We parked on the gravel near the farmer's stand and, with happy anticipation, inspected the many bushel baskets scattered about with all varieties of fruits and vegetables. Several people walked amongst the tables, checking the produce for ripeness and color. The farmer was a soft-spoken old man, wearing a red flanncl shirt and brown overalls. Strangely, he had on bright yellow tennis shoes. Finally, Mary and I decided to buy red apples, golden plums and corn. Mary also bought a cornstalk to decorate the patio of her home back in Olmsted Falls, Ohio. Without charging for the item, the farmer placed a small decorative squash into our bag and gave us a wink.

Back in the car now, our next stop would be the St. Francis Xavier Cemetery on Gallitzin Road in the little town of Cresson, not far from our Benscreek homestead. Our mother, father, and brother John were buried there. We visited their graves and, since we had no flowers, we laid an apple at each headstone. Mother died in 1942. She was buried on the first day of my senior year at Portage Township High School. It was Mary's first day as a freshman. Father was almost 14 years older than mother, and died twenty years after her, in 1962. Our brother John died in October of 1967. After saying a silent prayer for our beloved family members, Mary and I quietly walked back to the car and continued our drive.

At long last, we arrived at our sister Kay's home in Stumptown, a scenic suburb of Lilly, Pennsylvania. I believe the time has come to change the name from Stumptown to something a bit more apropos. Stumptown was probably appropriate when the first few settlers used their axes to good purpose, but it is now a lovely wooded area with several beautiful homes, and there is nary a single stump to be seen anywhere. Besides, Stumptown sounds much too close to Dumptown, which conjures an equally unappealing image.

Kay greeted Mary and me with smiles and hugs, relieved and happy that we had a safe trip. Soon we were seated at her cozy kitchen table with heaping plates of delicious Polish food: Potato pancakes, kiełbasa, gołumpki and pierogi. Kay's son Alan, an erudite professor, entertained his favorite aunts by giving us an update on his current classes, his insufferable students, and by reciting fragments of Shakespearean verse from a play that he soon would be directing for the school.

We could never sit down to a meal at Kay's without thinking of her gentle husband John Zajdel, gone for 20 years now. John usually welcomed all his relatives with a big pot of homemade soup and homemade kiełbasa and made you feel so welcome. He was a township road supervisor and, in the winter, he awoke at 3:00 AM and drove a plow truck to clear the snow covered county roads. In the summer, he planted dozens of evergreen trees on his property and would give a sapling to anyone in Stumptown or Lilly who needed one. He raised chickens and visited widows and many other needy families and gave them eggs, not only on Thanksgiving Day and Easter, but also during week days. He was not a man of many words, but his actions were benevolent and considerate.

After a night of refreshing slumber and a good breakfast, Mary and I donned our "walking in the woods" attire in preparation for our pilgrimage to the little village of Benscreek, our place of birth. I can honestly say that these articles of clothing would never be mistaken for our Sunday go-to-meeting outfits.

We told Kay we would be back in about 2 hours. We walked at a leisurely pace and a few minutes later we were already on Route 53 near the last house leading out of Lilly. An aging gentleman leaning on the porch railing of his house, called out to us, "Yuh lookin' for cans?"

Mary and I stopped, looked at each other, and then realized the uncomplimentary implications of his question.

"Hey, I guess we're not The Benscreek Beauties anymore."

"Speak for yourself," she told me. "He didn't see me. I'm walking on the other side of you. I told you to wear some nicer clothes."

"Well, I wore these junky clothes for my safety. I didn't want to look too enticing for fear some handsome stranger with dubious intentions might want to pick me up."

After a moment of embarrassment, the humor of the incident assailed us. We laughed so loud that tears ran down our cheeks. Undaunted, we pressed on.

Soon, the Scanlon Hill Road loomed before us.

As we clambered up Scanlon Hill Road, our breathing became more difficult and our hearts strained with the effort. When we got to the top of the hill, I remembered all the homes. I wondered where the families who lived there at one time had dispersed. I recalled the names of families like Pike, Brisini, Rimini, Krumenaker, and Van Blargen. But most of the homes were gone now. Where did the children of those families decide to live their lives? Did they ever return to Scanlon Hill? It was so long ago that I knew these woods, these roads, these families.

Prior to 1926, the year of my birth, my mother and father with their first four children, my brother Frank and my sisters Ann, Catherine, and Rose, had moved from nearby Jamestown, Pennsylvania, to a house on this very Scanlon Hill. My father had gotten a job in the Benscreek coal mine owned by C.A. Hughes Company. The Hughes mine was directly below Scanlon Hill, but then when winter came, it was a precipitous path down to the mine. My father learned from the Straw Boss at the mine that there was an old house in tiny Benscreek belonging to the mine which was unoccupied, but was lacking any type of utilities and in much need of repair. With a growing family, my parents decided to move there. I don't know how they managed to move yet again with their five children, one of them a newborn. Eventually, that little Benscreek house would witness the home births of four more Barnish children and one miscarriage.

As Mary and I gratefully began the sudden descent on the road to Benscreek, I told her about the evening, in the middle 1940s, when my girlfriend Margie Smolko and I walked three miles to the Lilly Dairy Dell, hopefully to attract the two handsome boys we had spotted the last time we were there. Almost no one had cars in that area in those days, so we walked. Windblown and tired, we stopped by the Stone Church on the corner and combed our long hair, then entered the Dairy Dell. We were sorely disappointed as Johnny and Tootie were nowhere to be seen. We listened to the wonderful jukebox music -- Artie Shaw, Glenn Miller, Duke Ellington, Harry James, Guy Lombardo, Woody Herman, and songs like Chattanooga Choo Choo, Tuxedo Junction, In the Mood. After dancing two jitterbugs with each other, as the local girls had already snatched up the other guys, we decided to head for home as it was already getting dark.

Mary said, "Gee, that was too bad, Sophie, that you didn't see Johnny. I always knew you liked him. Didn't his family own the grocery store across the street?"

I told her that was the one.

"Did you and Margie thumb a ride home?"

"Heavens, no!" I said. "And we were scared to death! It was pitch dark, with no moon. There are no houses by the side of the road all that way on 53 and we still didn't get to Scanlon Hill where it is just as deserted. When we finally got to Scanlon Hill, it was so dark we imagined that every tree had a monster hiding behind it and every bush had a crouching ghoul ready to jump on our backs."

"I'm glad I wasn't there," Mary whispered, and then smiled, "Tell me more."

I told Mary the rest of Margie's and my scary walk back home to Benscreek those many years ago. Margie and I had just made it to the top of Scanlon Hill when we heard two obviously inebriated men walking up the road, singing *Oh My Darling, Clementine* at the top of their lungs. We leaped over the guardrail and skooched down in the bushes until they disappeared from sight. Without streetlights, the darkness can play games with your eyes and your mind. We were young, but we were careful.

"It's a lucky thing you and Margie didn't roll down the hill and crack your skulls on those big boulders down that steep hill and land a mile down in the crick," Mary said excitedly.

"Well, I find no cowardice in playing it safe. We got home happy and safe that night."

At last Mary and I came to the bottom of the Scanlon Hill. I knew what was there and I knew it was time for a dam story. A swimming dam story. Mary pointed into the woods toward where the swimming dam used to be. To get to the swimming dam in the summers, we walked barefoot on the scorching hot, iron train tracks and a few times got splinters from the old wooden railroad ties. On the sweltering days when everyone wished they could just dive in or bellyflop right into the water, we knew better. That water was frigid. Even on days when the air temperature hovered in the eighties, we would stand for quite a while by the edge, dipping only our toes because the water was so icy cold. Then the local prankster boys would sneak up behind us and push us into the water. We shrieked and feigned shock and anger, but in reality, we liked the attention. After about two minutes, we climbed back out because our lips turned blue and we got goose pimples. Then we'd make a dash to lie on the large flat boulders nearby as a means to stop shivering. It's funny how no one brought a towel to lie on, but towels were a luxury in the thirties. At home, rags were used as towels, unless company came. Then and only then would mother bring out a fancy towel which she had embroidered with a pretty flower or lamb. I still treasure the one Mother and our sister Ann embroidered showing Jesus as a shepherd with the embroidered words, *The Lord is my Light and my Salvation.*

"Remember that kid, Paulie somebody?" Mary asked me. "He was always at the swimming dam. I think he liked you."

"I know. As soon as he saw me, he'd chase me with that dead snake. I'd jump in the water, shrieking my head off. It was dead, but it was a snake! He always hid that dead snake in a bush somewhere, waiting for the next time he saw me come up the swimmin' dam."

After our joyful reminiscing about the good old days at the swimming dam, we came to our childhood schoolhouse, now the Benscreek Social Club. It warmed my heart to know that it is still not dilapidated, but used for celebrations and other civic meetings and social gatherings where the local residents can come to enjoy their lives. We decided to go inside.

As soon as Mary and I walked in, the aroma of freshly baked pizza made our eyes glow with anticipation. We stood inside and looked around to find a familiar face, and soon as the mists of the years lifted, we recognized a few faces. In turn, we were recognized by old classmates and neighbors. It was so nice seeing them again with their grown children. Our pizza was soon served. As we sat enjoying our delectable lunch, I told Mary I was positive that my school desk, when I was in 7th grade, was exactly in the very spot where we were now sitting.

Mary talked about her school days, and a friend named Peggy. Mary was looking forward to visiting her in nearby Oil City.

But first we wanted to walk on the ground where our childhood home once stood.

Our tiny Benscreek home was built by my father and his cousin, Mike Golden from nearby Wilmore, in the early 1930s. Father and Mr. Golden knocked down most of the original old mining house, but kept two of the lower rooms to the house. Because my oldest brother Frank was already out of the house and working for Franklin D. Roosevelt's Civilian Conservation Corps (CCC), and Ann and Kay were working as maids in New York, the two lower rooms would eventually become a bedroom for mother and father, and a bedroom for baby Stanley. The new upstairs would eventually have two bedrooms: one room with two beds for me and my sisters Kay,

Rose, and Mary, the other smaller room for my brothers Joey and Johnny. Until the new house was completed, the five of us had our deluxe accommodations in the attic of the cow barn.

Yes, the cow barn.

The straw was warm and comfortable for us. However, the circumstance may have been uncomfortable for one being: Manya, the cow. She was probably disgusted with all the human noises above her head. She must have taken all the two-legged commotion in stride, as I did not hear her moo even once. I imagine that her bovine arrogance lifted her above our boorish intrusion into her stately position in the heights of animal society; she aloofly ignored our presence. Joey and Johnny couldn't stand Rose's and my giggling and straw flinging, so, as it was summer, they went to sleep outside under the grapevine.

Father and Mr. Golden were expert carpenters and the walls and the roof of the rebuilt house were soon finished. Our hayloft adventure was soon over.

As Mary and I walked across the Benscreek baseball field to get to our birthplace, I said, "Remember when our Benscreek batters would hit the ball in our yard? It was an automatic third base hit." Mary added, "And Mother would tell us to run upstairs and *open* the windows in the two front bedrooms above the porch to keep them from being broken." Mother was always worried about that. Fortunately, the upstairs windows were hinged to open completely to the inside of the rooms. Oftentimes, when standing in our kitchen, we would hear a ball hit our house, and more than once, we would hear a ball bouncing on the wood floor above us.

Mother loved the ball games, as children, friends, and many spectators from all the little towns came to have a good time. Cars would line the ballfield and the drivers and occupants would cheer and honk their car horn whenever a homerun was hit, or a great play was made. One year, the Benscreek baseball team was the Cambria County League champions. A tall pole was erected in left field near the fence on our property and the championship flag was hoisted. The event made the front page of many of the county newspapers, with several large photos of our hometown heroes. Some of the opposing teams came from the towns of Colver, Revloc, Puritan, Nanty Glo, and Ehrenfeld, the hometown of the Hollywood actor Charles Bronson.

But, the ball field was empty now. Where were the cars and the honking horns? Where were the happy children?

When we got to our house, tears of sadness replaced our smiles. The house was gone. Was it just a dream? Where was the front porch? And the coal stove? And the flowers that my mother so lovingly nurtured? Where were the fruit trees planted by my father? Where were the fences that he built with his own coal-smudged hands? Where was the Rock Garden Wall, built from the boulders and rocks which my father and Joey and Johnny hauled up the hill from the crick in the hollow down below? What had stood as a labor of love had disappeared, as if it was never there, a mirage, a fable, a fantasy, a myth.

Like so many simple, wood and shingle birthplaces in the Alleghenies, time took its toll. Time erased my birthplace. My parents died. The children moved on. The nieces and nephews moved on. Many years before, the title passed hands. The family still owned the lease on the land, but, back when the title was transferred, even then there was no reason to repair what remained.

Mary and I found two ceiling boards lying in the weeds where our house once stood. They were from our upstairs bedroom. We took the boards as a token of remembrance.

Mary and I respectfully and solemnly walked the grounds. The leaves in the hardwood trees in the hills above us were a fire orange and yellow. We sat on the large boulder which is still, after all these years, under what remains of the old grapevine trellis. We recalled our happy childhood. Almost every memory began with, "Remember when?"

We reminisced about mother the most.

We knew that time had marched on and the world had changed. We had changed. Our hair and hands and gait were testament to that. But in our hearts and minds, we were still young, and Benscreek, Pennsylvania, was still a small coal mining town, vibrant with poor but happy families and happy children just like us.

The Barnaś (Barnish) Family
of Benscreek, Pennsylvania

Jan Barnaś
b. 1-5-1883
in Ochotnica, Galicia, Poland
d. 5-7-1962

Arrived in America (Ellis Island)
4-17-1903 on the *S.S. Patricia,*
sailing from Hamburg, Germany

Maryanna Czajka
b. 10-4-1896
in Ochotnica, Galicia, Poland
d. 8-27-1942

Arrived in America 1911
(Baltimore?)

Frank
b. 9-19-1915
d. 1-20-1964

Married:
Grace Louder

Children:
- Frank
- Betty
- Janet
- Dorothy
- James

Catherine
b. 11-4-1918
d. 7-25-1995

Married:
John Zajdel

Children:
- Casimir
- Thomas
- Alan

Joseph
b. 10-4-1922
d. 2-11-2009

Married:
Ruth Castleberry

Children:
- Jo Nan
- Peggy Lee

Ann
b. 8-26-1917
d. 2-3-2004

Married/Divorced

Children:
- None

Rose
b. 11-4-1920
d. 8-5-2012

Married:
Joeseph Yanik

Children:
- Gloria
- Joyce
- David

Gertrude Sophia
b. 2-22-1926

Married/Divorced

Children:
- Donna
- Robert

Stanley
b. 3-30-1932

Married
Joan Frathellos

Children:
- Margo
- Christopher
- Athena

John
b. 5-10-1924
d. 10-13-1967

Married:
Helen Koken

Children:
- Rick
- Mary
- Michael

Mary DeLane
b. 11-20-1928

Married:
Medio Caucci

Children:
- Medio
- Barry
- Marina

Made in the USA
Middletown, DE
25 May 2021